BENJAMIN FRANKLIN

BENJAMIN FRANKLIN
SCIENTIST AND INVENTOR

BY EVE B. FELDMAN

FRANKLIN WATTS
NEW YORK | LONDON | TORONTO | SYDNEY
A FIRST BOOK 1990

Cover courtesy of The Bettmann Archive

Photographs courtesy of: The Bettmann Archive: pp. 13, 15 right, 16, 18, 32;
Franklin Technical Institute: pp. 14, 15 left; Historical Picture Service:
pp. 17, 39, 53 top; Photo Researchers: pp. 21 (Lowell J. Georgia),
27 (Phil Jude/Science Photo Library), 28 (Kent Wood); Rutgers University:
p. 23; Philadelphia Museum of Art/Mr. and Mrs. Wharton Sinkler Collection:
p. 37; Cigna Museum and Art Collection: pp. 35, 50, 51, 55; Jeff Greenberg:
pp. 43, 49, 53 bottom; Bausch and Lomb: p. 46.

Library of Congress Cataloging-in-Publication Data

Feldman, Eve.
Benjamin Franklin, scientist and inventor / Eve B. Feldman.
p.   cm.—(A First book)
Summary: Discusses Benjamin Franklin's experiments and inventions
involving electricity and examines his improvements to everyday
objects of his time.
Includes bibliographical references.
ISBN 0-531-10867-8
1. Franklin, Benjamin, 1706–1790—Juvenile literature.
2. Scientists—United States—Biography—Juvenile literature.
3. Inventors—United States—Biography—Juvenile literature.
[1. Franklin, Benjamin, 1706–1790.   2. Scientists.   3. Inventors.]
I. Title. II. Series.
·Q143.F8F45   1990
509.2—dc20
[B]
[92]
90-12191   CIP   AC

For Joel, my twentieth-century universal man

The author would like to acknowledge Roy Goodman of the American Philosophical Society.

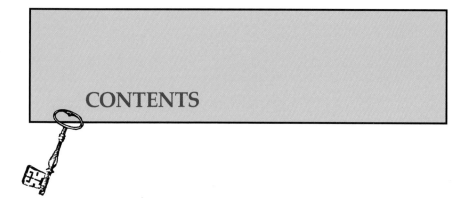

CONTENTS

Chapter One
FRANKLIN THE SCIENTIST
11

Chapter Two
ELECTRICITY
20

Chapter Three
POSITIVE AND NEGATIVE
25

Chapter Four
THE KITE
29

Chapter Five
THE LIGHTNING ROD
34

Chapter Six
FRANKLIN THE INVENTOR
40

Chapter Seven
OTHER INVENTIONS AND FIRSTS
48

Experiments You Can Do
with Static Electricity 57

Glossary 60

For Further Reading 62

Index 63

BENJAMIN FRANKLIN

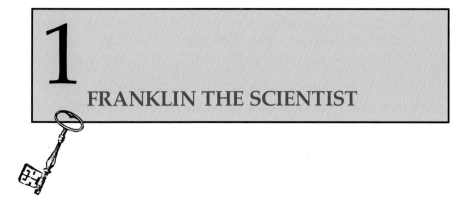

1

FRANKLIN THE SCIENTIST

Benjamin Franklin never watched television. He never listened to the radio, saw a movie, or played computer games. He never even turned on a light switch. When Benjamin Franklin lived, more than two hundred years ago, none of these things existed. That's because televisions, lights, radios, and computers are all powered by electricity. And in Franklin's time, no one knew very much about electricity: what it was, where it came from, or how to use it. In fact, it was Benjamin Franklin's curiosity that made him study and experiment with electricity.

In 1706 when Benjamin Franklin was born, people used candles to provide light. This was good for Benjamin's father, Josiah Franklin. He was a candle and soap maker in Boston.

Even though people needed candles, Benjamin's father was not a rich man. He had a large family to support. Benjamin, his youngest son, was the fifteenth of seventeen children. The Franklins couldn't afford to give Ben more than two years of school, so Ben only went to school between the ages of eight and ten. His teachers probably didn't expect him to become famous. It's likely that they just hoped he'd finally understand arithmetic, in which he did very poorly.

But Benjamin Franklin was a *scientist*, even as a young boy. He was always trying to find out why things were the way they were. And he was always trying to make things better.

As a boy, Ben experimented with all kinds of tricks to improve his swimming. Once he held on to a kite while floating, and let the kite pull him across the water. He also made himself wooden paddles to see if they would make him a better swimmer. The paddles for his hands, called pallettes, had a place for his thumbs. The paddles on his feet were sandal-like flippers. Ben decided that the paddles were too heavy to help him swim.

Of course, no one knew Ben was a scientist then. They just thought he was full of curiosity. It was curiosity that made Benjamin Franklin an avid reader. He wanted to know everything about

*Although Ben disliked the work in his
father's candle shop, he stayed with it for
two years. Later in life he said that this
work taught him how to handle tools.*

everything, and he thought that the best way to do that was to read books. Ben said he couldn't remember a time when he wasn't reading. And he kept on reading, even after he had to leave school and go to work.

In those days, children started working at an early age. They learned a profession by working for someone whose trade they wanted to master.

Ben Franklin worked hard in Boston, learning how to operate the printing presses and how to sell the results.

Because Ben was so fond of books and reading, it was decided that he would learn to be a printer. He would be an *apprentice*, a kind of student-worker, for his older brother James.

Ben was a hard worker and he learned fast. He used his lunch time to read and teach himself as much as possible. He taught himself math. He even experimented on improving his writing.

By the time he was seventeen, Ben Franklin felt he'd learned quite a bit about printing. He wasn't getting along with his brother as his boss, so he left Boston and made his way to Philadelphia. He had barely any money, but he knew his trade. He found work as a printer's assistant and after several years of hard work, he opened up his own printing shop.

Before long, Ben combined his printer's trade with his writing talents. He bought a newspaper called the *Pennsylvania Gazette*.

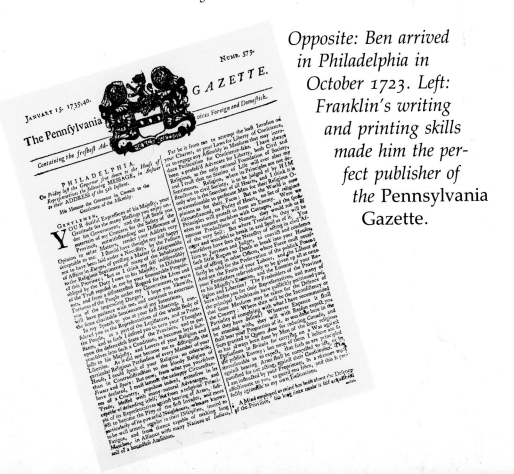

Opposite: Ben arrived in Philadelphia in October 1723. Left: Franklin's writing and printing skills made him the perfect publisher of the Pennsylvania Gazette.

Franklin also wrote and printed his own book called *Poor Richard's Almanack*. It came out once a year, full of practical advice, good humor, and lively sayings. It was very popular and helped make Benjamin Franklin a wealthy man. By the age of forty-two, Ben decided that he was rich enough to retire. He wanted free time to explore his many and varied interests, he wanted time to *experiment*.

Although Ben Franklin loved books and reading, he gave up his printing career to do other things.

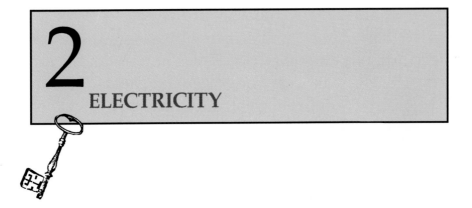

2 ELECTRICITY

Benjamin Franklin was watching a "magic" electricity show in 1743. A man named Dr. Spencer was performing tricks with what we call *static electricity*. (This is the kind of electricity that sometimes causes you to get a small shock when you walk on a carpet and touch a doorknob—or touch someone else—especially on a dry winter day.) Dr. Spencer performed stunts, such as drawing sparks from the hands and feet of a boy who was dangling from the ceiling by a silk cord. The audience applauded. Afterward, Ben Franklin spoke to Dr. Spencer. He wanted to know why these tricks worked. Dr. Spencer admitted that he didn't really understand why or how the tricks worked.

*Static
electricity
is what sometimes
makes your hair
stand up instead
of lying flat on
your head.*

But Ben Franklin was so excited by what he saw that day that he decided to investigate the subject himself. After he retired from printing in 1748, he devoted the next five years to electricity.

Franklin began his experiments with very simple equipment. He used a thick glass tube about two feet long, and a piece of leather or silk. He used the leather to rub the glass tube. This rubbing charged the tube with static electricity.

Later, Franklin used a kind of friction-maker, or glass-rubbing machine, that made it faster and easier to get sparks of electricity. This machine was a simple wooden stand that held a big glass jar. A handle was attached to one end of the jar. When you turned the handle, the jar turned. As it turned, it rubbed against a piece of material that sat on a platform under the jar, and this produced static charges. The jar also touched metal prongs that leaned against the top of it. This machine was called an *electrostatic* machine, because it made a lot of static electricity.

Franklin was able to capture and store these charges in another simple device called a *Leyden jar*. A Leyden jar was just a plain glass jar with a tin-like foil wrapped around the bottom of it, both on the inside and the outside. Water was kept in the jar, and the jar was closed by a cork stopper. A metal rod went through the cork, straight into the water in the jar. If you touched this rod to the metal from the electrostatic machine or to the rubbed glass tube, the static electricity traveled down the rod and was captured inside the jar. Then, touching the rod at the top of the jar would produce big electric shocks and sometimes sparks.

Franklin wasn't satisfied just using the Leyden jar to capture electricity. He wanted to know what

This mechanical toy from about 1770 shows Ben Franklin in the act of discovering electricity.

made this jar such a good collector of electricity. Franklin planned a series of experiments to find out what part of the Leyden jar was the most important part: the metal rod, the water, the foil, or the glass bottle. Carefully, one at a time, he separated and tested each of these parts. He discovered that the electricity was held in the glass.

This made Franklin ask another question: Did the glass need to be shaped like a bottle? He planned a way to find out. He would electrify a different piece of glass, one that didn't have a bottle-like shape. Franklin took a flat windowpane and put a thin sheet of lead on each side of it. With his friction-maker, he passed static electricity sparks to both pieces of metal. Carefully, he removed both sheets of metal. Neither metal sheet had any electricity in it when it was by itself. But the glass did. This simple series of experiments gave the world some very important information. Franklin had built something called a *condenser*. A condenser stores electrical charges. But he couldn't find anything practical to do with this condenser. Other scientists, many years later, benefited by Ben Franklin's discovery. The condenser is used in every modern electrical device: radios, televisions, telephones, refrigerators, etc. Ben Franklin was ahead of his time.

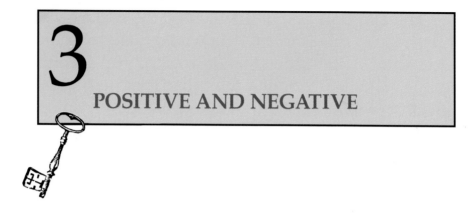

3

POSITIVE AND NEGATIVE

Imagine the excitement of discovering something so new that you would have to make up new words to describe it! This is what happened when Benjamin Franklin tried to find out where electricity comes from. He found that there are *positive* and *negative* charges. He was the first person to use these words to describe electricity.

Franklin was trying to see in what direction electricity traveled. He designed a simple experiment using three men. Two of the men stood on blocks of wax, so that they would be *insulated* from the ground. (That means that any electricity that they held would not pass out of them to the ground, where it would be lost.) Franklin knew that electricity did not easily pass through wax.

Franklin gave one of the men on the wax a large glass tube to rub. This rubbing would build up static electricity in the tube. Franklin asked the second man on the wax to touch the tube. That man got a shock. Franklin watched as the three men seemed to "pass" the static electricity shocks through their fingers. There was a spark when each of the men on the wax touched the man on the ground. But then the electricity passed to the ground. There was an even bigger spark when the men on the wax touched each other. But once they did that, neither one had any more electric charges to pass around.

What did it mean? Where had the electricity come from? What was making it travel from one person to another? Franklin said that electricity was not created. He decided that electricity was like a *fluid* that is everywhere and in everything, all the time. He said that all objects had the same amount of this electric fluid until something, such as rubbing a glass rod, made some of this electric fluid pass from a person to that rod. Then, the glass rod would have more fluid than it normally had, and the person who did the rubbing would have less fluid than he or she normally had. According to Franklin, electric sparks or shocks occurred when

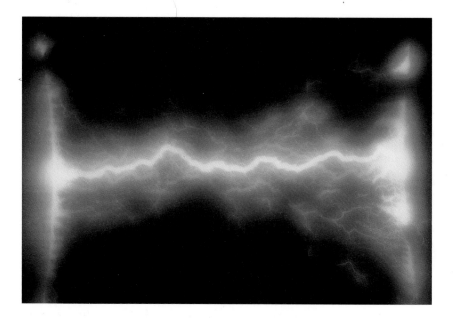

*This photo shows an electrical discharge
between two metal objects.*

this electric fluid passed between objects that had
unequal amounts of electric fluid. Franklin used
"positive" and "negative" to describe the differ-
ences between more and less than the normal
amount of electricity.

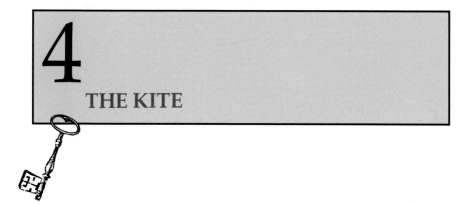

4

THE KITE

In 1752, Benjamin Franklin performed his most famous experiment. It was an extremely dangerous experiment. Franklin had an idea, a theory. He believed that lightning was a form of electricity.

Many people disagreed. They thought that lightning was a display of heavenly power. But Franklin wasn't just guessing when he suggested that lightning was electricity. He based his idea on serious observation. He wrote down a list of ways that lightning and electricity were alike. This list included the fact that both electricity and lightning give light, both create light of a similar color, both travel in a crooked direction, both make noise, and both can start fires.

The idea that lightning was electricity was a very daring idea for those times. In fact, when members of the Royal Society in England, an English scientific society, read what Franklin had written about lightning being electricity, they laughed. Franklin did not let their laughter stop him. He was determined to test his idea.

But how would he prove his theory? You couldn't just take a ladder and climb up and touch the sky to see if you would feel a shock. Touching lightning is a sure way to get killed! Franklin thought and thought and finally decided to try to reach the lightning by using a kite. If he flew a kite in a storm, and the kite became electrified, it would prove his theory.

Lightning is deadly. Franklin knew that. He planned his experiment carefully, and enlisted the help of his son, William. William was about twenty-one years old at the time, and he too understood the risks.

Franklin made the kite by attaching a large silk handkerchief to two crossed bars of wood. He used silk because he thought that a regular paper kite would be destroyed in a storm. To the top of the kite, he attached a sharp, pointed wire. In his earlier experiments, he had discovered that pointed metals attracted electric charges. To the bottom of the kite, Franklin attached the usual string or twine that one would use to fly a kite, and to that he attached a long silk ribbon. He used a silk ribbon because he knew that silk was not a good "passer," *conductor*, of electricity. Franklin knew that if he held on to the silk ribbon, he would be safer.

Lastly, Franklin tied a metal key to the spot where the string and the silk ribbon were joined. He used the key because it was metal and it would be a good conductor of electricity. It would be a spot to test for the presence of electricity in the kite. If there was electricity in the kite, the experiment would prove that electricity came from the lightning.

Franklin's plan was to hold on to the silk ribbon and stay under cover, so that the silk would not get wet in the storm. He knew that if the silk was wet, it would no longer be safe to hold it. Water is a very good conductor of electricity.

As the storm began, William ran to send up the kite. Then he joined Franklin in the safety of a small shed. The kite flew up to the storm clouds.

Franklin was worried that his experiment had failed, until he noticed that some of the fibers of the kite's string were standing on edge. They were standing up, just the way static electricity made hair and fibers stand up! With great care, Franklin

reached out toward the key. As his knuckle touched the key, Franklin received a shock. His experiment had worked. The shock he felt proved that electricity had traveled through the kite to the key. Lightning was electricity. (Franklin was very lucky that the kite had not been hit by a bolt of lightning. If it had, the shock would have killed him.)

When the kite and its string were all wet and full of electricity, Franklin used the key to draw the electricity into a Leyden jar.

Franklin described his experiment and his conclusions in writing. In simple language, in his own newspaper, he explained how to perform this experiment. Scientists all over the world read his report eagerly. Ben received many awards and became famous in America and in Europe. The Royal Society of London, the same people who had laughed at him before, awarded him their highest honor, the Copley Gold Medal. Harvard and Yale universities also gave him honorary degrees.

Ben Franklin's
famous kite experiment
validated his theory that
lightning was electricity.

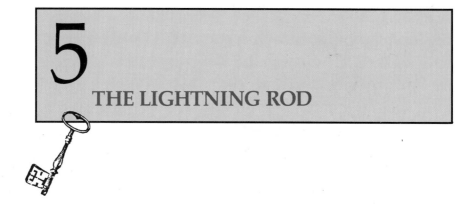

5
THE LIGHTNING ROD

Fame and medals were not Franklin's goal in experimenting. He wanted to know the "why" of things and he wanted to use his answers to make life better. Now that he knew that lightning was electricity, he would use what he knew about electricity to try to control lightning. He would try to prevent the many terrible fires that started when lightning struck buildings. Franklin turned from investigator to inventor. He designed a very simple device called the lightning rod.

In planning this device, Franklin used information that he had learned from his electrical experiments. He had concluded that electricity was more attracted to pointed objects. And he knew that metal was a good conductor of electricity. So

*Franklin's life was filled with questions
he tried to answer through experiments.*

when he proved that lightning was electricity, Franklin came up with a simple way to control it. He suggested attaching a pointed metal rod to the top of every home and public building and connecting these rods to the ground. Electricity would hit the rod and pass safely to the ground, without hitting and damaging the buildings, or anything that could catch on fire.

Franklin shared his invention with the world. He described it in letters to England. And in the 1753 *Poor Richard's Almanack* he published clear and simple instructions on how to make such a rod.

Benjamin Franklin did not invent electricity. No one invented electricity. What Benjamin Franklin did was to suggest that electricity isn't magic and that it exists all around us. Franklin's experiments showed what electricity was like. His ideas about electricity were so new that there weren't words to describe them. Franklin had to invent his own words. Some of the words first used by Franklin

Angels assist Ben Franklin
in his experiments with
electricity in this nineteenth-
century oil painting.

about electricity are: battery, conduct, conductor, plus, minus, condenser, positive charge, negative charge, electrician, electric shock.

Franklin wanted to improve things. That's why he used the results of his experiments to design the lightning rod. He also suggested that electric shocks were a less terrible way to kill animals than other means. He tried to kill a turkey this way and nearly died himself from the shock. Franklin also tried to use electric shocks as medicine. But his experiments did not convince him that such shocks were any real help to sick people. He worried that electricity might not be very useful after all.

Franklin gave up his electricity experiments to take jobs that his country asked him to do. He was Postmaster General for all the colonies. He spent many years as a diplomat, a representative of the American colonies, first in England and later in France. He helped write the American Declaration of Independence and the Constitution. His work was very important to the birth of the United States of America. (You may wish to read about this part of Franklin's life in other books.) But this book will continue to tell you only about Franklin's life as a scientist and as an inventor. Even though he gave up his work with electricity, Franklin continued to contribute to the advancement of science all his life.

Franklin helped draft the Declaration of Independence. He was a great statesman, and lived his beliefs in his personal life as well, as this letter to a former friend attests.

Philada July 5. 1775

Mr Strahan,

You are a Member of Parliament, and one of that Majority which has doomed my Country to Destruction.— You have begun to burn our Towns, and murder our People.— Look upon your Hands!— They are stained with the Blood of your Relations!— You and I were long Friends:—You are now my Enemy,—and

I am,

Yours,

B Franklin

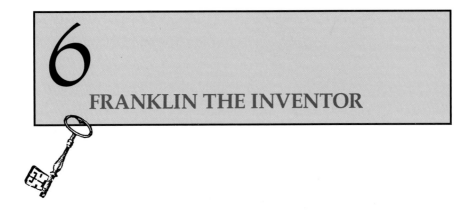

6
FRANKLIN THE INVENTOR

THE FRANKLIN STOVE

Benjamin Franklin invented a stove. It was not a cooking stove, but a type of heater.

Before this invention, people who wanted to keep warm had to sit close to a fireplace. The hot air from the fire did not travel beyond the fireplace, and much of that hot air was lost as it went up the chimney. It was especially hard to sit right near the fire in public places like inns (restaurant/hotels in Franklin's day). There wasn't room for everyone to get close enough to the fireplace. Once, when Franklin was traveling around the country, he stopped at an inn. It was cold but there was no room by the fireplace. Benjamin Franklin went up to the owner of the inn and announced in a loud voice that he wanted a bucket of oysters for his horse. The owner of the inn was surprised by that order. He had never seen a horse that ate oysters before! Ben Franklin insisted that oysters be brought out for his horse. Everyone in the inn ran outside to see the horse that would eat oysters. When everyone got up, Franklin took the opportunity to find himself a comfortable space, right by the warm fireplace. His horse didn't eat the oysters, but Franklin had found a way to make himself warm.

Making people move out of your way was not a good solution to the problem. Benjamin came up with a better idea. He invented a "box," made of iron, which fit into the opening of the fireplace. The iron sides of the box got hot from the fire, and in turn, spread the heat around the room.

Franklin wrote and published a pamphlet describing this invention. It was called "An Account of the New-Invented Pennsylvania Fire Place." Benjamin Franklin could have made a great deal of money from this invention if he had taken out a *patent* on it. A patent registers an invention in the inventor's name and protects the inventor's right to be the only one allowed to make and sell the product. But Franklin didn't want a patent. He said that "as we enjoy great advantages from the inventions of others, we should be glad of an opportunity to serve others by any invention of ours, and this we should do freely and generously." He didn't call it "The Franklin Stove" either. He called it the "Pennsylvania Fire Place," but it soon became known as the Franklin Stove.

THE ARMONICA

Benjamin Franklin's talents also touched the world of music. Franklin had taught himself to play the guitar, the harp, and the violin. And he loved listening to music that others made.

One day in 1761, when he was in England, Franklin went to an unusual concert. The musician, Edmund Delavel, didn't play the piano, the harp, the guitar, the violin, or the organ. He played glasses filled with water! The glasses were made of crystal, which is a very fine type of glass. Each one was filled with a different amount of water. Mr. Delavel played them by wetting one of his fingers and rubbing it around the rim of the glass. Each glass produced a different beautiful note. Mr. Delavel played songs with this simple rubbing.

Ben Franklin enjoyed the concert. He liked the unusual sound of the music, but he wanted to im-

The Franklin Stove (left) distributed heat around a fireplace, warming an entire room. Franklin's armonica (right) is on display at the Independence National Historical Park in Philadelphia.

prove this glass-playing. He wanted to be able to play several notes at the same time. Franklin thought and thought. He had an idea: What if instead of rubbing glasses with different amounts of water in them, he would rub wet glasses of different sizes?

Franklin went to a glass maker and ordered thirty-seven glass bowls, in twenty-three different sizes. He asked the glass maker to put a hole in the bottom of each bowl. Franklin took the bowls home and tested them. He ground off a little glass from the bowls that didn't sound perfect. Then he painted the rims so that highs and lows of the same note would have the same color. (All Cs were red, all Fs were green, and so on.) Next Franklin put all the bowls in size order, lying on their sides. The bowls were carefully put in a row, to overlap but not touch each other. Next, Franklin slid an iron rod through the holes in each bowl to connect them—just like stringing beads. Then he attached the rod to a wheel, and connected the wheel to a foot pedal. When the pedal was pushed the wheel turned, the rod turned, and the bowls turned.

Franklin wet the bowls with water and a sponge. Then he wet his fingers and rubbed the glass rims. His foot kept the bowls turning. It worked. What lovely sounds! With practice, he could play more than one note at the same time, the way a pianist plays the piano. Franklin called his musical invention an *armonica*, an Italian word (meaning harmonies), in honor of Italian music.

Franklin enjoyed the armonica so much that he had a carrying case built for it. And he was not the only one who enjoyed it. It was a hit all over Europe. Famous composers like Beethoven and Mozart composed music for the armonica. Franklin composed music for it, too.

BIFOCALS

As Franklin got older, he had a problem. He needed two pairs of eyeglasses: one for seeing things at a distance, and a second pair for seeing things close up.

Franklin was already wearing spectacles (glasses) for distance viewing. He didn't like carrying two pairs of glasses. Often he wished he could be wearing both glasses at the same time. This was especially true when he was eating. He wanted to see what he was putting into his mouth, but he also wanted to see the people sitting across from him. This problem particularly bothered him in France. He explained that when you are listening to and speaking a foreign language, it helps to see the face of the person who is speaking to you.

At the age of seventy-nine, Franklin's scientific mind suggested a solution. Why not cut both pairs of eyeglasses in half crossways, and put each half

I therefore had formerly two Pair of
Spectacles which I shifted occasionally
as in travelling I sometimes read and
often wanted to regard the Prospects.
Finding this Change troublesome and not
always sufficiently ready, I had the
Glasses cut, and half of each kind
associated in the same Circle, thus

together again to form a new circle? That way, if he always wore his glasses, he could look down to see things near, and look up to see things that were distant. His solution worked for him. And it still works for people today, more than two hundred years later. You probably know some adults who use *bifocals*; they look like a regular pair of glasses with a line dividing them in half.

Franklin's bifocals have given youthful vision to millions of people since their invention in 1784.

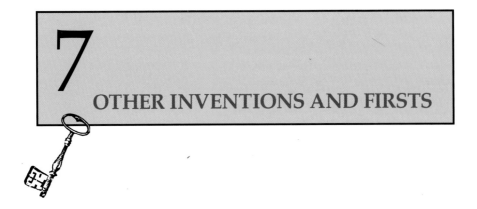

7
OTHER INVENTIONS AND FIRSTS

Did you ever see a long stick used like giant tweezers in a grocery store or a library to grab something from a high shelf? Benjamin Franklin invented that when he was eighty.

Is there a desk in your school that is actually a chair with a built-in writing table? Thank Benjamin Franklin for that, too.

Ever hear about lead poisoning? Do you know who was the first person to suggest that? You guessed it!

When you take a book out of your local library, you should think of Benjamin Franklin. As a young man in Philadelphia, he decided it was important to share books, and he came up with the idea of public libraries.

Franklin invented a chair that turns into a ladder when you flip over the seat.

He wrote about colds and the importance of exercise. What he wrote more than two hundred years ago sounds as modern and true as anything written today.

This dual-purpose chair is also a ladder!

Ben Franklin founded the Union Fire
Department, one of his many efforts to make
Philadelphia a better place to live.

Franklin replaced the round globes on street-lights with four flat glass panes. These lamps gave better light, and were easier to fix if one of the panes broke.

Did you ever notice that wearing light colors in summer helps you feel cooler? Franklin noticed. And he proved this with a simple experiment: He took different colored squares of material and placed them outside on the snow on a sunny winter day. He waited to see which colored square would sink into the snow first. It was the black square, because the black square absorbed heat instead of reflecting it. This caused the snow underneath it to melt and the square sank.

Franklin introduced new plants to America: Swiss barley, Chinese rhubarb, Newton apples, turnips, and willow for basket weaving.

The first political cartoon was created by Ben Franklin.

He suggested daylight saving time to save fuel.

In his eight trips across the Atlantic Ocean, Franklin noticed that the trip is much shorter from the United States to London than vice versa. He tried to find out why. Over the course of forty years, he carefully observed and measured the temperature of the water, and discovered something called the Gulf Stream. The Gulf Stream is a current that

Franklin even did research while traveling, and thus discovered the Gulf Stream. Maps of the Gulf Stream helped sea captains plot their courses.

runs through the Atlantic Ocean. Although sea captains were aware of the current, there were no maps of it. Franklin had charts drawn up for them so that they could take advantage of this knowledge.

Taking care of the land was also important to Franklin. He suggested planting clover to put nitrogen back in farmed soil. And he recommended using gypsum (a mineral containing calcium) as a fertilizer.

Benjamin Franklin was not a scientist with a laboratory full of equipment. He performed most of his experiments in his home. And he was not a scientist who devoted all his time and energy to scientific work. Benjamin Franklin was a universal man—a man who was busy and talented in many fields: writer, printer, publisher, diplomat, statesman. But Franklin was a scientist in the larger sense of the word. He was a man full of wonder and curiosity who tested everything around him to see

Ben Franklin was a man with many interests and many talents.

if he could understand it and make it better. And he used a scientist's care to test his ideas with carefully planned experiments.

Benjamin Franklin was also a man of great vision because he could imagine new inventions and new solutions. He kept on learning and inventing all his life, until he died, in 1790, at the age of eighty-four.

Franklin wrote that he sometimes wished he had been born later, to see what progress science might make in a thousand years. Many of Franklin's ideas and inventions have survived more than two hundred years.

Maybe in eight hundred years or so, technology will have people living in outer space, but they might still be wearing bifocals in the library.

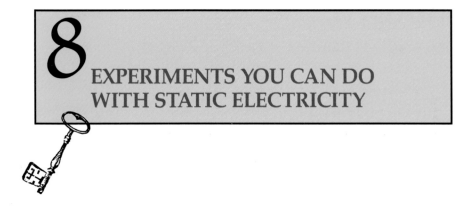

8
EXPERIMENTS YOU CAN DO WITH STATIC ELECTRICITY

(These experiments work best in cool, dry weather.)

CHARGING YOURSELF

Equipment: a rug, a radiator or doorknob

Shuffle your feet as you walk across a carpet. Touch something made of metal (doorknob, radiator). You should feel a slight shock. To test Ben Franklin's idea that pointed objects are more attractive to electricity, try this experiment with your finger and then with your fist.

BALLOON CHARGES

Equipment: balloons

1. Blow up a balloon and tie it closed. Rub the balloon against your clothes. Put the rubbed side against a wall. The balloon will stick to the wall for a while. Try sticking charged balloons to other things, including yourself!
2. Repeat the rubbing of a balloon. Put the balloon near your hair. See how the electrified balloon makes your hair stand up.
3. Rub a balloon until it is well charged. Hold it close to your ear. Do you hear little crackling static noises? These are the noises of tiny sparks that are jumping between you and your electrified balloon.

CHARGING A COMB

Equipment: plastic comb, piece of wool or nylon, piece of paper

Tear the paper into little bits. Rub the comb briskly with a piece of wool or nylon. (You may even be able to do this by rubbing the comb vigorously against your hair.) Then hold the electrically charged comb near the bits of paper. See the paper cling to the comb.

DRAWING A SPARK

Equipment: sheet of newspaper, plastic bag (like the kind used to wrap vegetables or used to send home clothes from the dry cleaners), smooth, round top of a can (at least 3 inches in diameter)

Put a dry sheet of newspaper on the table. Using the plastic, rub the newspaper vigorously to work up a good electrostatic charge. Put the metal piece in the middle of the paper. Lift the paper off the table by holding it on both sides. Have someone else quickly put his or her finger near the metal piece. You will see a harmless spark.

GLOSSARY

apprentice—a student who learns a craft or skill by working for someone who is an expert at that craft

armonica—a musical instrument made of glass bowls

bifocals—eyeglasses that allow for distant and close vision at the same time

charged—full of electricity

condenser—a device which holds or stores a charge of electricity

conductor—something that passes electricity along; water and metal are good conductors as electricity flows through them easily.

electrified—charged with electricity, full of electricity

electrostatic—having to do with static electricity

experiment—to try out a carefully planned test of an idea

fluid—like a liquid, something that flows

Gulf Stream—a warm current of water in the Atlantic Ocean; it flows from the Gulf of Mexico up the east coast of the United States and then across the Atlantic to Britain.

insulated—protected from electricity

Leyden jar—invented in Leyden, Holland, this was a glass jar, filled with water and coated with a tin-like foil; it was a good container for static electricity charges

negative—one of the two types of electrical charges (the other is called positive)

patent—a patent is an official document from the government that registers an invention in the inventor's name. This protects the inventor's right to be the only one allowed to make and sell the product.

positive—one of the two types of electrical charges (the other is called negative)

scientist—a person who tries to understand the world by careful observation and experiment

static electricity—stationary charges of electricity, such as those produced by friction, or rubbing

universal—interested and knowledgeable about a great many subjects

FOR FURTHER READING

Aliki. *The Many Lives of Benjamin Franklin*. New York: Simon & Schuster, 1988.

Cousins, Margaret. *Benjamin Franklin of Old Philadelphia*. New York: Random House, 1963.

Franklin, Benjamin. *Essays, Articles, Bagatelles, and Letters, Poor Richard's Almanack, Autobiography*. New York: Library of America, 1987 (with notes from J. A. Lemay).

Fritz, Jean. *What's the Big Idea, Ben Franklin?* New York: Putnam, 1982.

Graf, Rudolph F. *Safe and Simple Electrical Experiments*. New York: Dover Publications, 1973.

Meltzer, Milton. *Benjamin Franklin: The New American*. New York: Franklin Watts, 1988.

Sandak, Cass R. *Benjamin Franklin*. New York: Franklin Watts, 1986.

Scarf, Maggi. *Meet Benjamin Franklin*. New York: Random House, 1968.

Stevens, Bryna. *Ben Franklin's Glass Armonica*. Minneapolis, Minn.: Carolrhoda, 1983.

INDEX

Armonica, 42–45

Beethoven, Ludwig van, 45
Bifocals, 44–47

Chair-ladder invention, 49
Colors, 52
Condensers, 24
Conductors, 31
Constitution, U.S., 38

Daylight saving time, 52
Declaration of Independence, 38, 39
Delavel, Edmund, 42

Electricity:
    condensers, 24
    conductors, 31
    discharge of, 28
    experiments you can do, 57–59
    fluid, similarity to, 26–27
    lightning, 29–33, 34, 36
    positive and negative charges, 25–27
    shocks, uses of, 38
    static electricity, 20, 21–22, 24, 57–59
    storage of, 22, 24
    words about, 27, 36, 38
Electrostatic machine, 22
Eyeglasses, 54

Farming, 54
Fire fighting, 50–51
Franklin, Benjamin:
    awards for, 33

Franklin, Benjamin (*continued*)
    early years, 11–12, 14
    education, 12, 15
    final years, 56
    music, interest in, 42–45
    Philadelphia, move to, 16, 17
    political career, 38, 39
    printing career, 14–19
    reading, love for, 12, 14
    See also experiments and inventions
Franklin, Josiah, 11, 12
Franklin, William, 30, 31
Franklin Stove, 40–42, 43

Gulf Stream, mapping of, 52–54

Insulation, 25

Kites, 12, 29–33

Lead poisoning, 48
Leyden jar, 22, 24, 33

Libraries, 48
Lightning, 29–33
Lightning rod, 34, 36

Mozart, Wolfgang Amadeus, 45

Patents, 41
Pennsylvania Fire Place, 40–42, 43
Pennsylvania Gazette, 17
Political cartoons, 52
Poor Richard's Almanack, 19, 36

Royal Society of London, 30, 33

Spencer, Dr., 20
Static electricity, 20, 21–22, 24, 57–59
Stove for heating, 40–42, 43
Streetlights, 52
Swimming experiments, 12

Words about electricity, 27, 36, 38